The Ultimate
MAZE BOOK

Galen Wadzinski

Dover Publications, Inc.
Mineola, New York

Bibliographical Note

The Ultimate Maze Book is a new work, first published
by Dover Publications, Inc., in 2005.

International Standard Book Number

ISBN-13: 978-0-486-44535-9
ISBN-10: 0-486-44535-6

Manufactured in the United States by LSC Communications
44535612   2017
www.doverpublications.com

Introduction

This book contains seven different styles of mazes grouped together into separate sections. Each section starts out with simple instructions followed by easier warm-up mazes and progresses to more advanced mazes.

<u>3-D Construction Mazes (page 2)</u>: These mazes really are three-dimensional. Move along construction beams, climb up and down ladders and stairs, or try solving a truly four-dimensional maze.

<u>Over-Under Mazes (page 8)</u>: These mazes feature paths that go over or under other paths. Throw in a few restrictions, like one-way travel, and these mazes can be very challenging.

<u>Surface Mazes (page 14)</u>: Travel along the surfaces of cylinders and cubes. The surfaces are transparent, so both the front and back sides can be seen at the same time!

<u>Designated Stops Mazes (page 20)</u>: These mazes have designated stops along the way. You must enter and leave a stop on different paths. This leads to extremely-hard-to-solve mazes. The opening at which you enter a stop is critical. Don't just take the easy route.

<u>Key Mazes (page 26)</u>: Traveling through these mazes requires special keys to open locked doors. This unique twist leads to some very interesting mazes.

<u>Directional Arrow Mazes (page 30</u>): Bounce around these mazes by following arrows in a straight line, moving from point to point.

<u>Path Arrow Mazes (page 35)</u>: Follow arrows this way and that way, sometimes circling back on an arrow in the opposite direction.

Each maze contains an indication of how difficult it is to solve. A picture of a brain with varying amounts of gray matter appears in the upper right corner for each maze. An empty brain indicates the easiest mazes, while a full brain indicates the hardest mazes.

"No-Brainer"   "Overload"

The easier warm-up mazes will generally take only a few minutes to solve. Solving the warm-up mazes will help give clues on how to go about solving the more advanced ones, so don't skip them. The more difficult mazes could take many hours to solve.

The answers are on pages 39 to 46. There should only be one right answer for any given maze. If you have an answer that is different from the one in the book, go back and make sure you are following all the rules for that maze.

3-D Construction Mazes

This section contains 3-D-style mazes. Before you start a maze, it may be helpful to look at the maze for a while, until you get a feel for the 3-D view. For the beam-style mazes, it doesn't matter what side of the beam you are on. Think of yourself as an ant that can crawl on any side of the beam. See below.

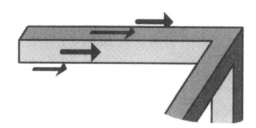

Valid and invalid paths:

The left image below is an example of a valid path. Starting on the top horizontal beam you can travel to the right behind the vertical beam. The top horizontal beam and the vertical beam do not touch. Remember to think "three-dimensional." To the right is an example of an invalid path, since the beams do not touch.

1. Construction 3-D

Help the ants find food. See the section introduction on page 2 for help on 3-D mazes.

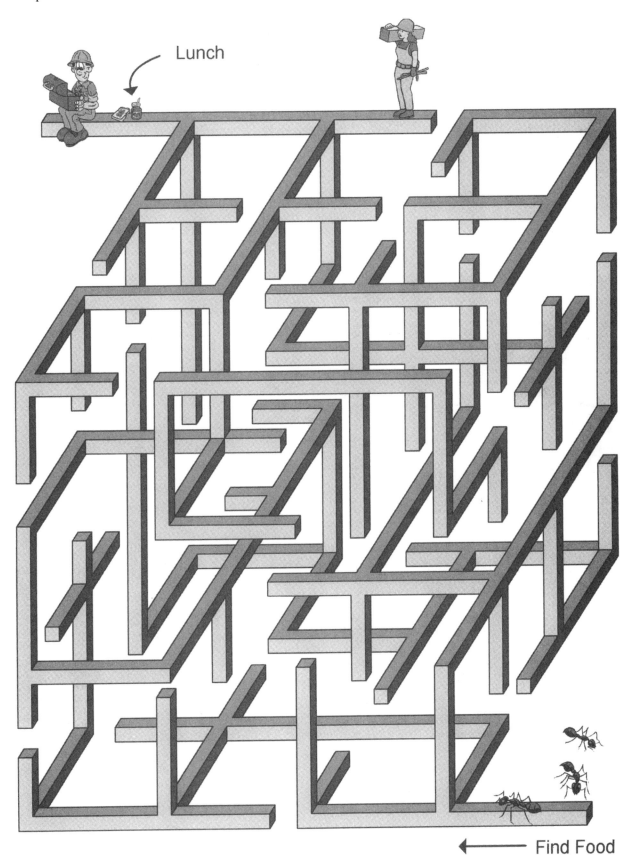

Lunch

← Find Food

This maze has a few loops in it, allowing you to travel in circles. Find the shortest path from "S" (start) to "E" (end). See the section introduction on page 2 for help on 3-D mazes.

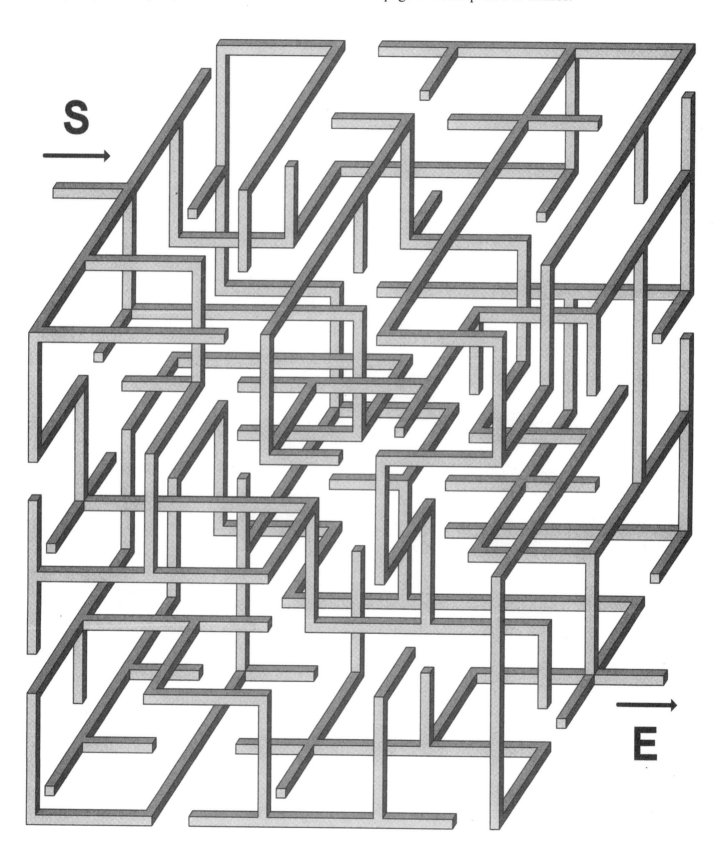

3. Three Planes with Ladders

Start at the "S" (start) on the top plane and go to the "E" (end) on the bottom plane. Use the ladders to travel between the planes, moving either up or down.

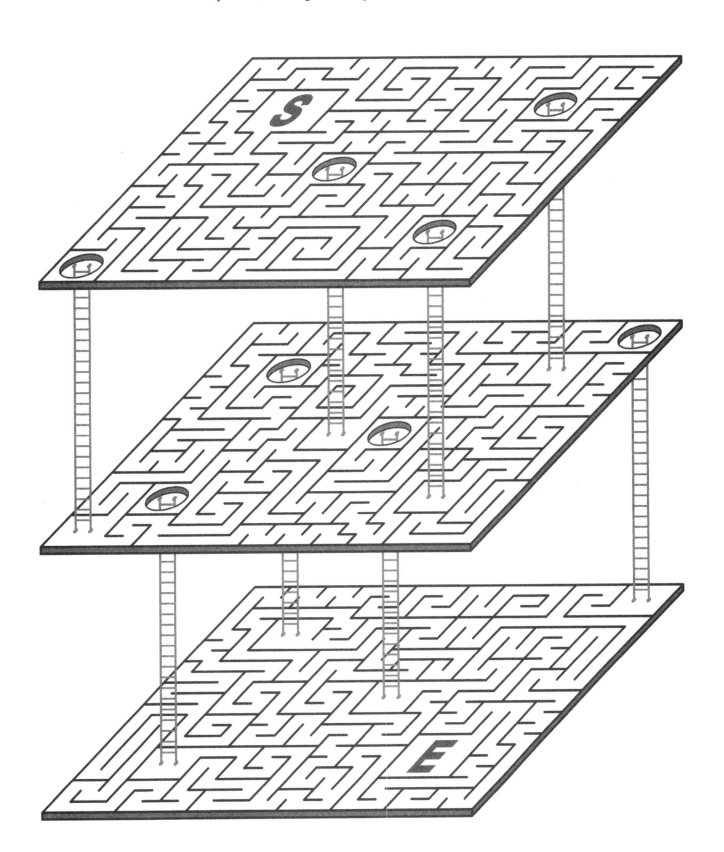

4. Four-Dimensional Maze

This maze consists of two 3-D mazes; one has shaded bars and the other has clear bars. The only places you can jump between the mazes are at the dark disc-like conduits (these conduits make up the fourth dimension). Start at the "S" and end at the "E". See page 2 for help with 3-D mazes.

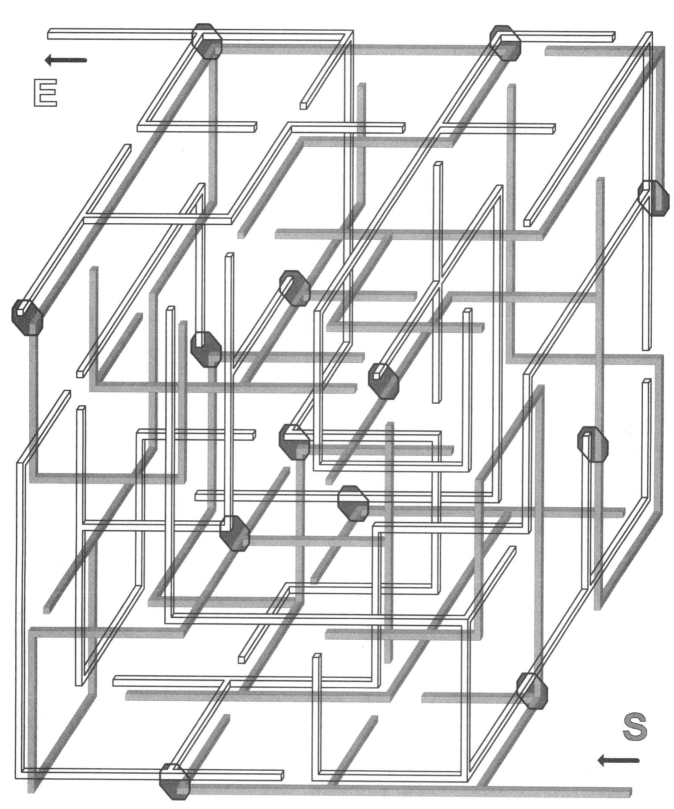

6

5. 3-D Walkways

Start at the "S" and take either the top path or the bottom path. End at the "E" in the lower right corner. Climb up or down stairs as needed. See the section introduction on page 2 for help with 3-D style mazes.

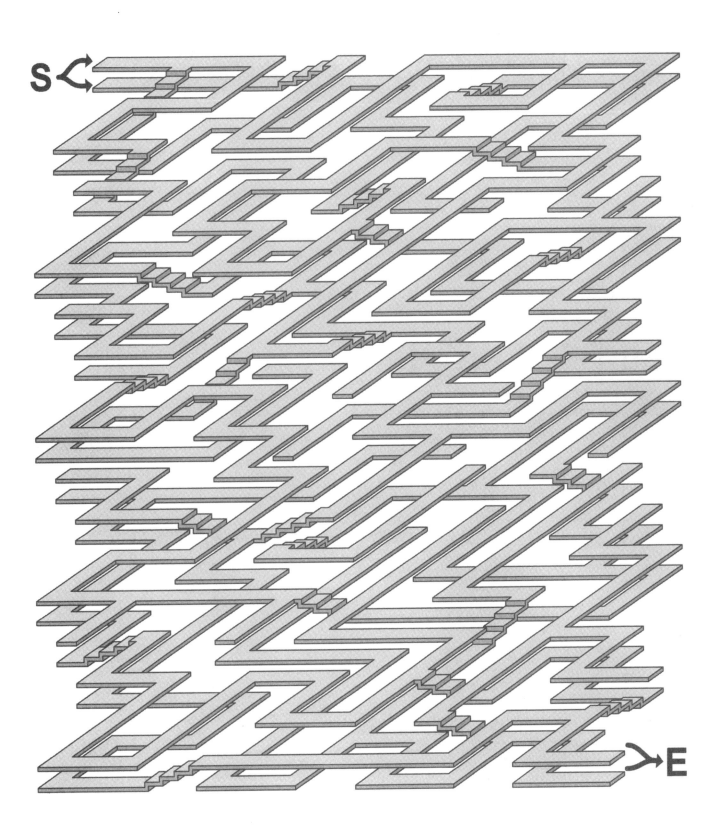

Over-Under Mazes

Definition

Over-Under mazes are mazes where the paths may go over or under other paths. Paths that go over or under another path are considered separate paths. In other words, you can't travel from one path to the other.

No U-Turns

In all the mazes in this book, unless otherwise noted, you can't make U-Turns. If you are traveling in one direction you can't just stop and turn around.

"No U-Turns" Signs

In addition to the "No U-Turns" listed above, there may be an added restriction on what path you may take. A double arrow >> at an intersection restricts movement around the corner indicated. This is also referred to as a "No U-Turn" sign.

One-Way Arrows

One-way paths are indicated with an arrow. You may not travel against an arrow.

Note:

Even though a maze may have "No U-Turn" signs, it may be possible for you to travel back on your own path in the opposite direction without making a U-Turn.

6. Anthill

Help the ants at the top of the anthill find their way to the nest at the center of the maze. For help with Over-Under-style mazes see the section introduction on page 8.

7. Deliver the Goods

Drive the truck with the supplies to the factory. Remember to watch for "No U-Turn" signs. See the section introduction on page 8 for detailed instructions on Over-Under mazes.

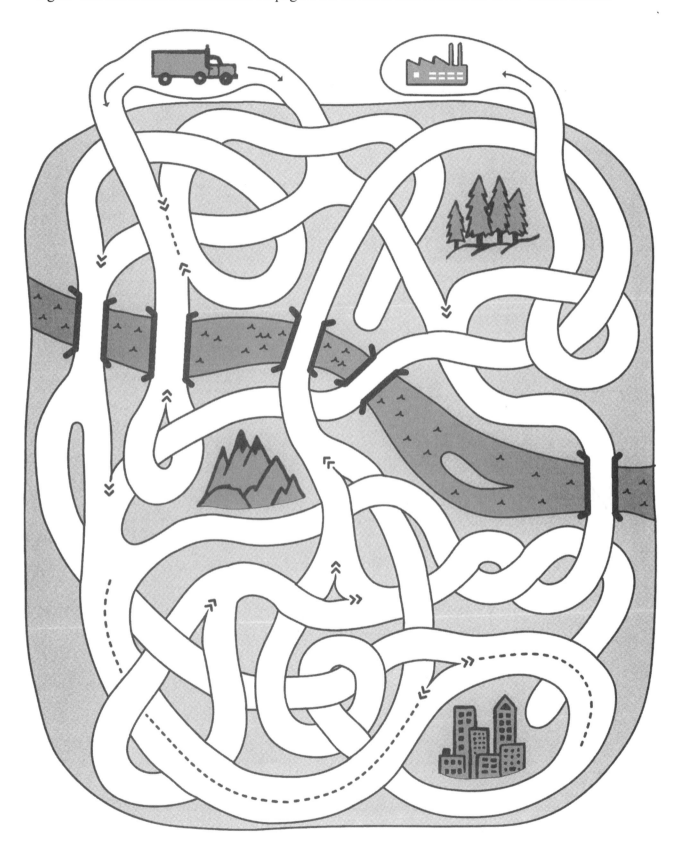

8. Blood Flow

Start in the left ventricle and find the path that leads back to the heart. See page 8 for help.

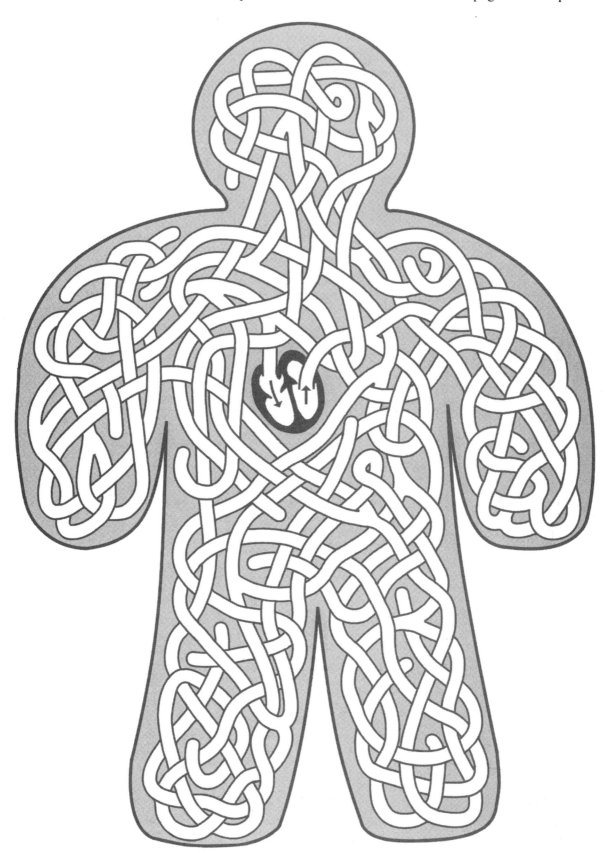

9. Weave

Start at the "S" and end at the "E." See page 8 for help with Over-Under-style mazes.

10. Commuter Madness

1. Start at home and commute to work. Obey the one-way streets and No U-Turn signs.
2. Travel from work back home. Again, obey the one-way streets and No U-Turn signs.
   See the section introduction on page 8 for detailed instructions on Over-Under mazes.

Surface Mazes

These mazes feature paths on the surface of either a cube or a cylinder. The image is transparent so both the front side and the back side can be seen. The mazes have clear paths and shaded walls. The paths on the back side are outlined with dotted lines and the paths on the front side are outlined with solid lines. This is to help you distinguish between the two sides. One helpful hint: move slowly through these mazes, since it is easy to get confused and jump from back to front or vice versa, when moving too fast. These mazes have their front-side surfaces shaded a little darker than their back-side surfaces, to help in distinguishing the two sides.

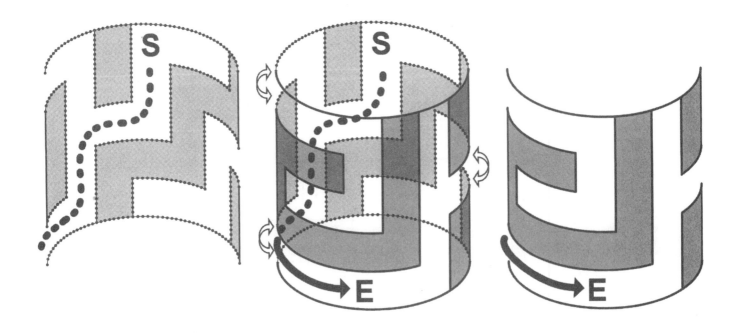

Above is an example of a cylinder maze. The image in the center is the actual maze with the solution path shown. The image to the left is what the back side of the cylinder looks like and the image on the right is what the front side looks like.

11. Cube Warm-Up

This maze is a warm-up to transparent surface mazes. Start at the "S" on the top of the cube and end at the "E" on the bottom of the cube. The cube at the center is the actual maze. The six sides of the cube are also expanded out so you can easily see the path on each side. The paths on the back sides are outlined with dotted lines and the paths on the front sides are outlined with solid lines. Move slowly to help keep your place. See the section introduction on page 14 for help with surface-style mazes.

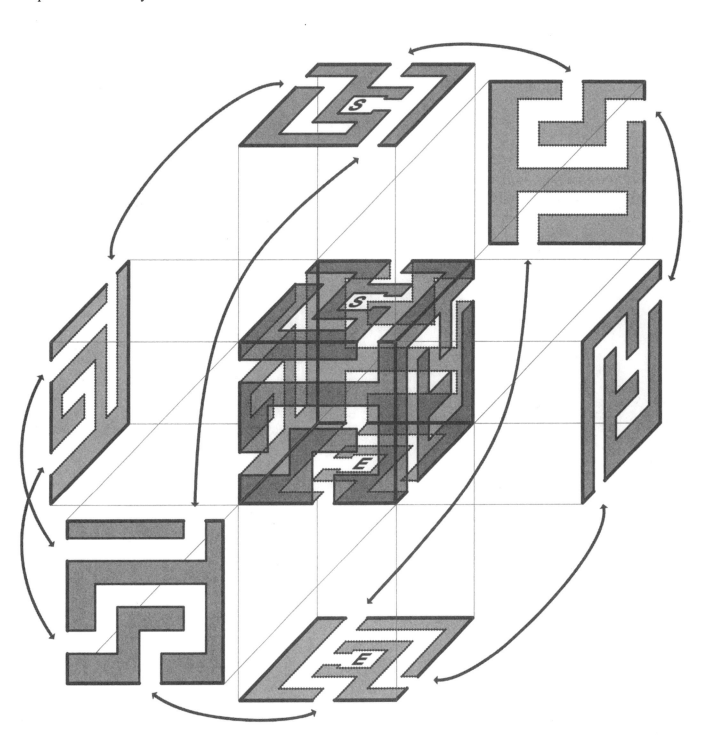

12. Cylinder Surface

Start at the "S" and end at the "E." This transparent maze has a clear path and shaded walls. The path on the back side of the cylinder is outlined with a dotted line and the path on the front of the cylinder is outlined with a solid line. See the section introduction of page 14 for help.

13. Die Surface

Start at the "S" and end at the "E". Although this maze is not a transparent-surface maze, it fits well into this section.

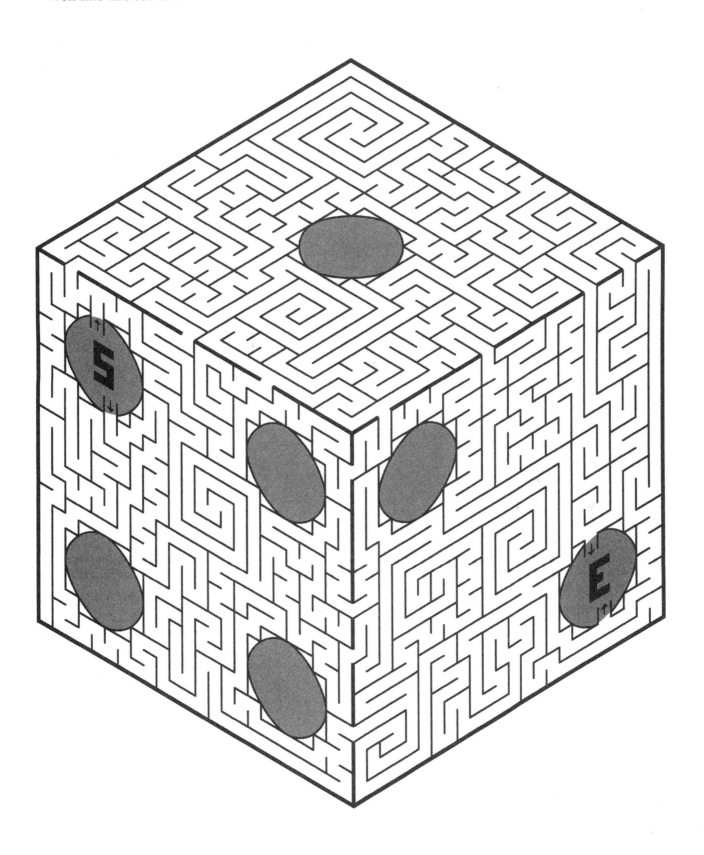

14. Cube Surface

Start at the "S" and end at the "E." This transparent maze has a clear path and shaded walls. The path on the back side of the cube is outlined with a dotted line and the path on the front of the cube is outlined with a solid line. Move slowly to help keep your place. Be careful to obey the one-way arrows. See the section introduction on page 14 for help with surface mazes.

15. Cube Surface

(4 mazes in 1)

1) Find a path from 1 (top) to 6 (bottom), without traveling through any other number.
2) Find a path from 2 (front) to 5 (back), without traveling through any other number.
3) Find a path from 3 (right) to 4 (left), without traveling through any other number.
4) Start on any number and travel to each of the other numbers in any order and then return to where you started. Do not travel through any number more than once. You must exit a number on a different path than the one you entered on. When you return to the number you started on you must enter it on a different path than the one you left on. See the Designated Stops section on page 20 for help.

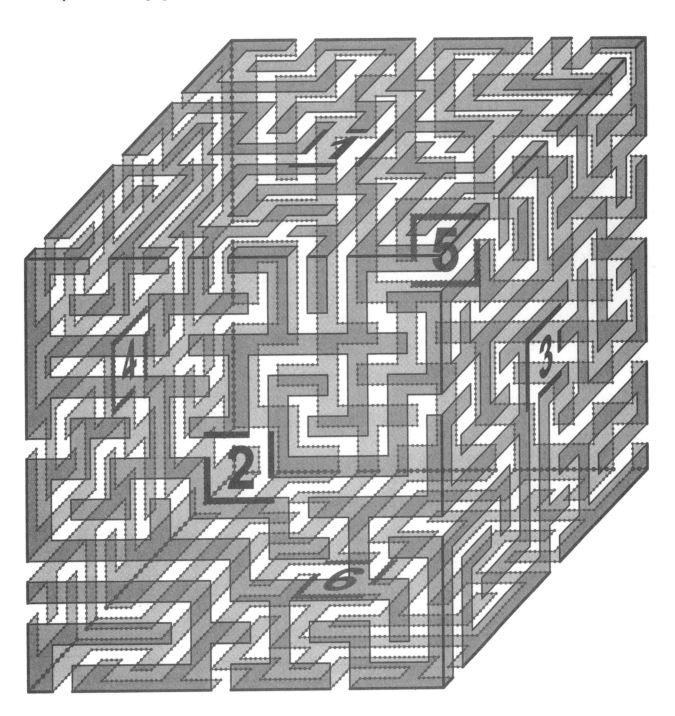

Designated Stops Mazes

This section is made up of mazes that contain designated stops. Designated stops are locations you must travel to. Some of the mazes will require you to visit these stops in order, while others will let you travel to them in any order.

Valid and invalid stops:

1). Whenever you make a designated stop you must exit on a different path than the one you entered on. The first picture below shows a valid path. The second picture shows an invalid path, since you are entering and exiting on the same path

2). You may not reenter a designated stop once you have already been there. The picture below shows an invalid path, since the path reenters the "A" stop after it has already gone through it.

3). Note that it may be possible to travel back over your path. The picture below shows an example of how you could end up traveling over your prior path.

16. Easy as 1- 2 - 3

Start at #1, go to #2 and end at #3. Remember that after you have entered #2 you must leave on a different path. See the section introduction on page 20 for help on mazes with designated stops.

17. Compass

Start at the center, either just to the right of the needle or just to the left of the needle. Then travel to all four directions of the compass in the following order: North, South, East and West ("N," "S," "E," "W"). Remember to exit a stop on a different path than the one entered on. See the section introduction on page 20 for help on mazes with designated stops.

18. Home Run

See if you can hit a home run. Start at home base "H," run in order to 1st, 2nd, 3rd and back to home base. You must leave a base on a different path than the one you entered on. See the section introduction on page 20 for help on mazes with designated stops.

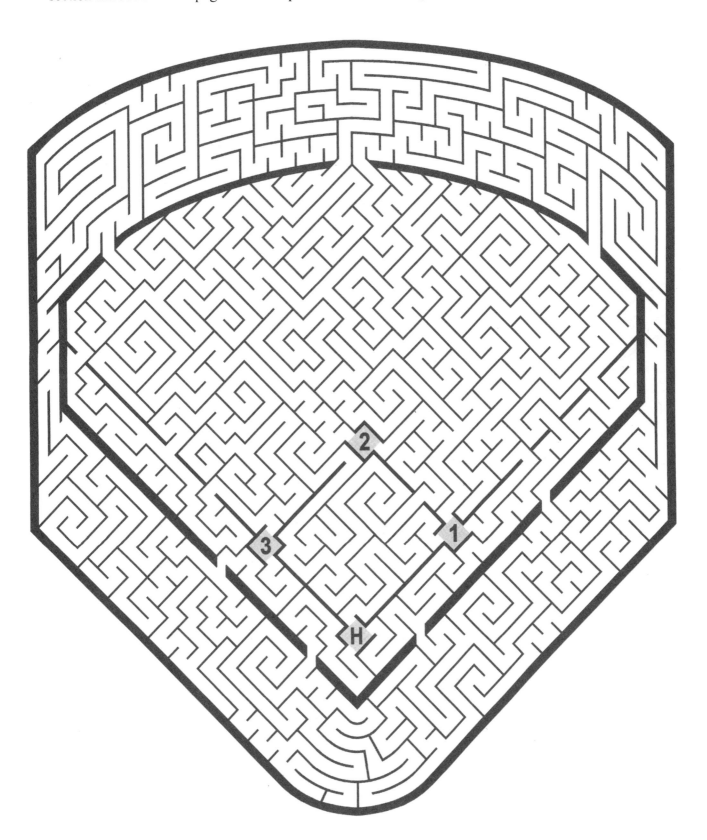

19. Cubes with Seven Stops

Start at #1 and proceed to the other numbers in order, ending at #7. Remember that after you enter a number you must leave on a different path. See the section introduction on page 20 for help on mazes with designated stops.

20. Pick up Kids

Start at the top. Drive the bus, picking up all the children; then bring them back to school at the top. See the section introductions on pages 8 and 20 for help.

Key Mazes

All of these mazes have the objective of finding "Fido" the dog and leading him outside to safety. The mazes have either rooms or apartments that contain locked doors, which can only be opened with the right key. Once inside a room or building you can exit through any door, as the doors are only locked from the outside. The following is a detailed set of rules:

- You can only carry one key at a time.
- As you pass by a key you don't have to pick it up.
- U-Turns are OK. You can pick up a key, turn around and head back the way you came.
- Once you pick up a key, the one you were carrying is thrown out and disappears.
- Doors are locked from the outside and you need the right key to open them.
- Once inside a room you can exit at any door you wish, no matter what key you are holding.
- Once you exit a room, the door you left by closes behind you; it doesn't stay open.

In addition to making a challenging puzzle, these rules allow you to solve the maze without having to keep track of numerous details. All you need to know is where you are in the maze and what key you are holding.

The maze below has an example of a valid path starting on the left and exiting at the wall in front. The path starts by picking up the #1 key and does a U-Turn back on itself, it then passes by the #3 key without picking it up. It then opens the #1 door to the room at the center. Once through, the door closes. Note that rooms will have dark thick walls. The path leaves the room through the #3 door, then that door closes. This is possible because you can always exit rooms through any door, no matter what key you are holding. The path then picks up the #2 key, throwing away the #1 key, and continues on through the front wall.

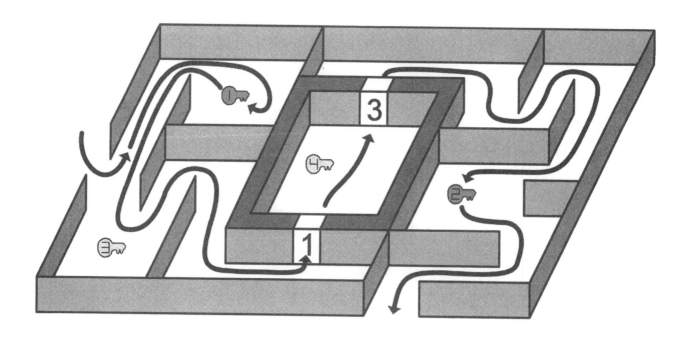

21. Jailbreak

A quick review (see also section introduction on page 26):

- Enter the dog pound. Find "Fido" and lead him outside to freedom.
- Pick up keys to open locked doors (you don't have to pick up every key you walk by).
- You can only carry one key at a time. When you pick up a new key, the key you are currently carrying is thrown out.
- Doors are locked from the outside. Once inside a room you can exit through any door.
- Doors will automatically close after you walk through them.

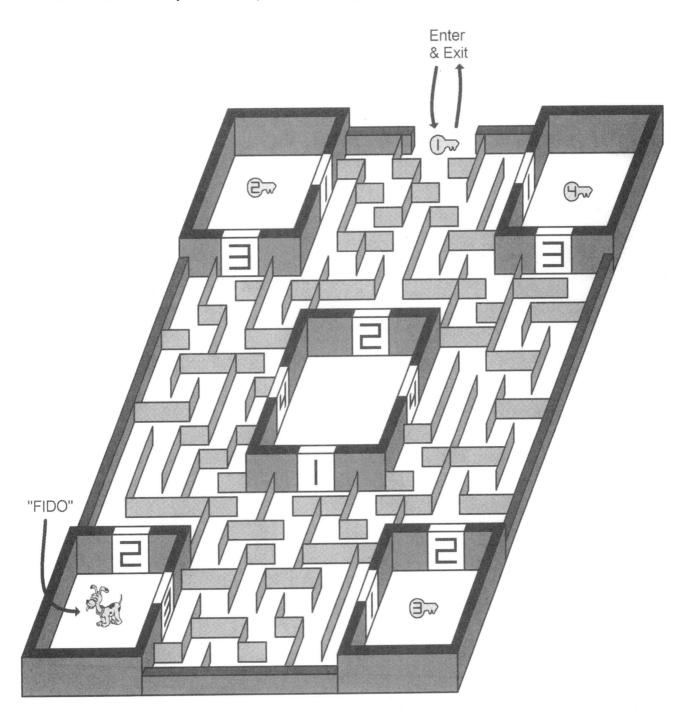

22. Mansion

A quick review (see also section introduction on page 26):

- Enter the mansion. Find "Fido" and lead him outside.
- Pick up keys to open locked doors (you don't have to pick up every key you walk by).
- You can only carry one key at a time. When you pick up a new key, the key you are currently carrying is thrown out.
- Doors are locked from the outside. Once inside a room you can exit through any door.
- Doors will automatically close after you walk through them.

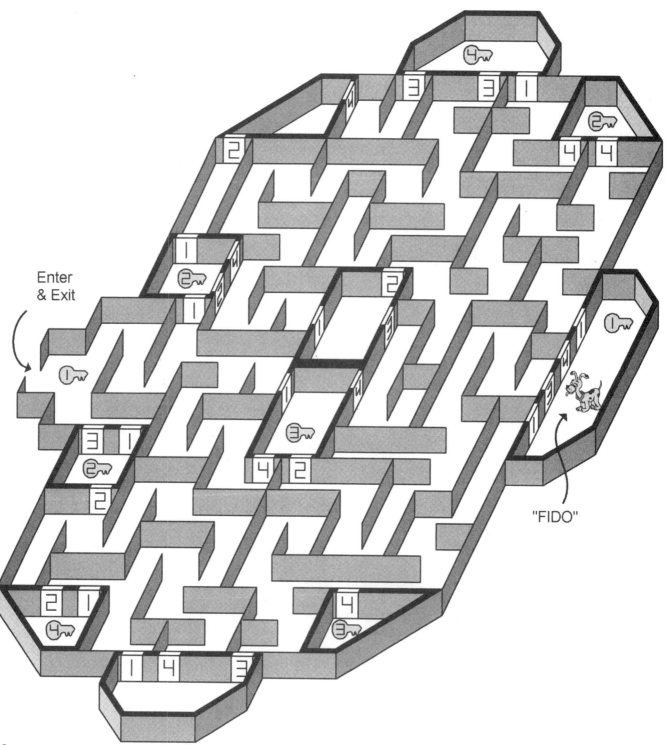

23. Building Fire

A quick review (see also section introduction on page 26):

- Enter the building. Find "Fido" and lead him outside to safety, avoiding fire areas.
- Stairs that are on fire have been shaded and cannot be used.
- Pick up keys to open locked doors (you can only carry one key at a time).
- Doors are locked from the outside. Once inside an apartment you can exit through any door.

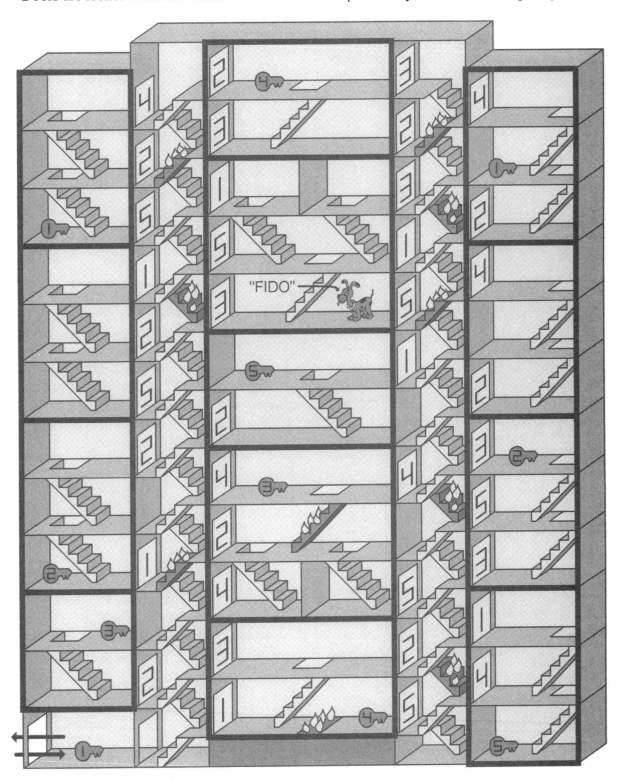

Directional Arrow Mazes

Each Directional Arrow maze includes instructions on where to start and where to end. After starting, proceed in a straight line until you run into an arrow or group of arrows. Choose one of the arrows and proceed in that direction in a straight line until you run into the next arrow or group of arrows. Continue until you reach the finish.

Below and to the left is an example of a valid path that starts in the upper left corner and ends in the lower right corner. To the right is an invalid path. Once you run into an arrow or group of arrows you must stop and follow a new arrow.

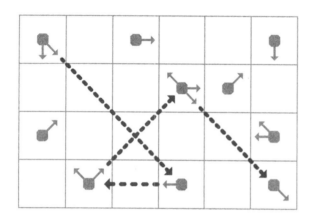
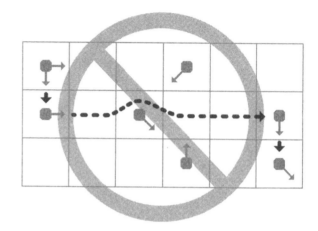

Only the solution path in a Directional Arrow maze will have an ending. All other paths will eventually end up in an infinite loop. Below is an example of a path that is in an infinite loop. Any node that is part of an infinite loop cannot be part of a unique solution. Therefore, if you find yourself traveling to a node you already visited, you might as well start over.

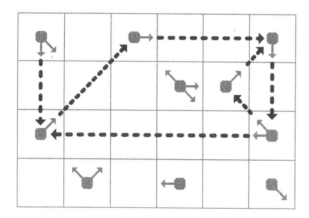

24. Chessboard

Start with the Queen in the upper left corner. Follow one of the arrows until you run into a pawn. Follow an arrow from that pawn to the next pawn. Continue following the arrows until you reach the King in the lower right corner. See page 30 for more detailed instructions.

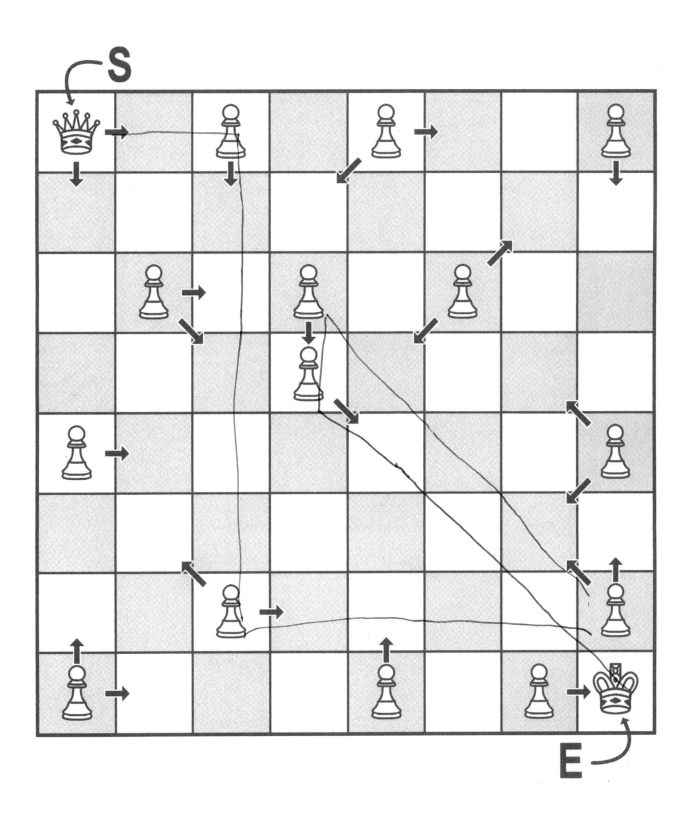

25. Trick Shot

Start by hitting the cue ball (unnumbered) and follow the arrow until you hit another ball. Continue following the arrows until you eventually hit the 8 ball into the lower left corner pocket. When you hit a side rail you bank off it. The first ball you will hit will be the 10 ball off a bank shot. If you run into one of the other pockets, you missed and will have to start over. Watch out for the side pockets; it is easy to think you can bank off them. See page 30 for detailed instructions.

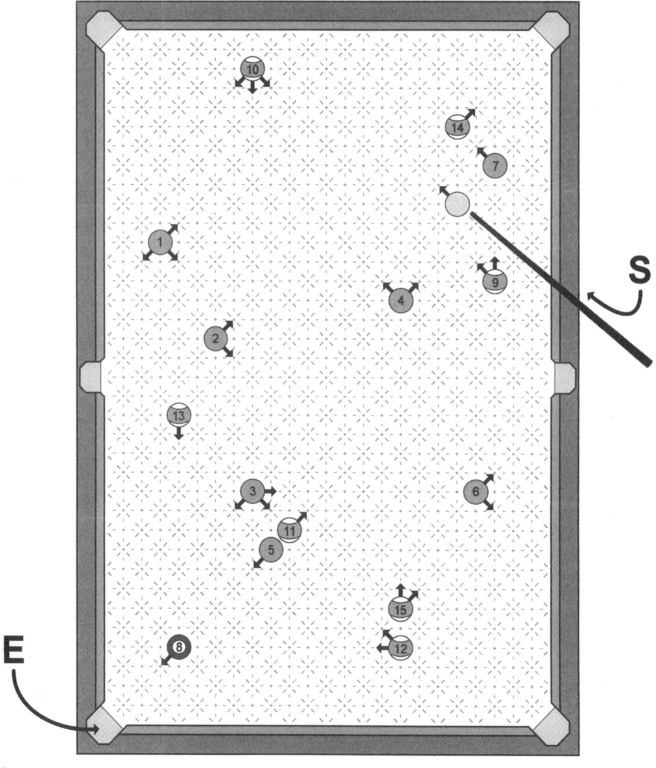

26. Hexagonal Arrow Maze

Start at the "S" at the upper left and follow the arrows to the "E" in the upper right. See the section introduction on page 30 for detailed instructions on Directional Arrow mazes.

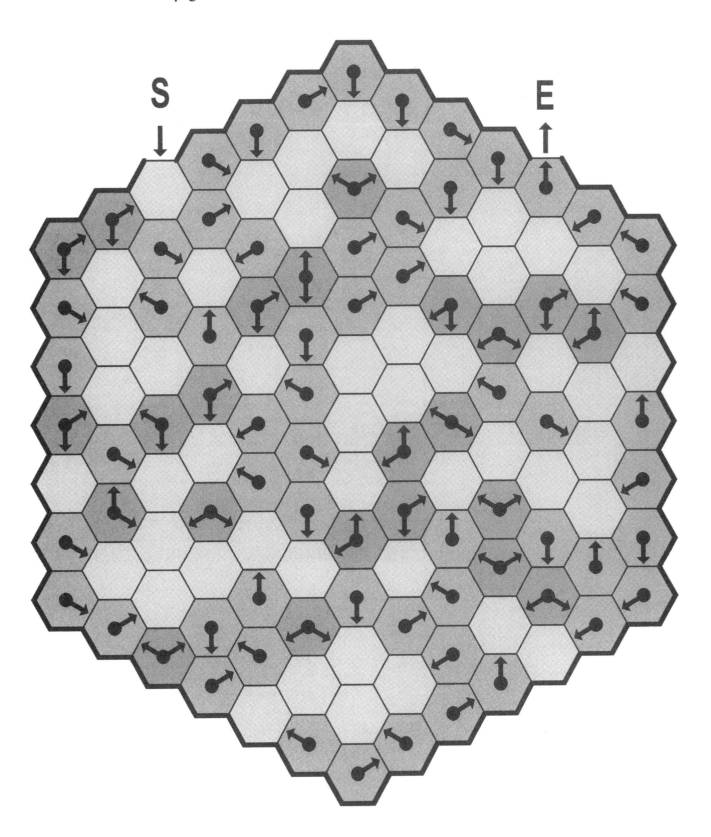

27. Lone Electron

Help the lone electron at the top left make its way to the atom at the center. Bounce in a straight line from atom to atom, following the arrows. See the section introduction on page 30 for help.

Path Arrow Mazes

These mazes are solved by following arrows. The arrows may follow a straight path or a curved path. The example below on the left shows two valid paths. Notice that you can travel against the head of an arrow that is pointing in the opposite direction, as long as there is an arrow pointing in the direction you are traveling. The example below on the right shows two invalid paths. Although the top path follows a curved arrow, it is pointing in the wrong direction. The bottom path doesn't have an arrow that curves from the left and points down.

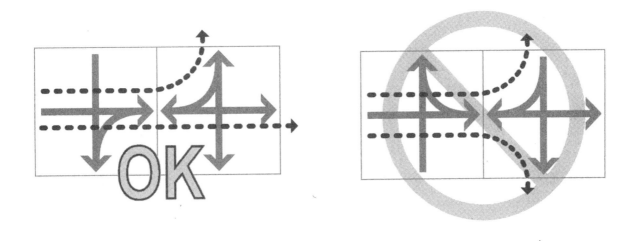

You can't make U-Turns and turn back on your path, as in the example below and to the left. Even though you can't make U-Turns, it may be possible to double back on your path. Below and to the right is a valid path that doubles back on itself.

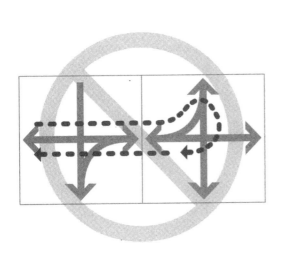

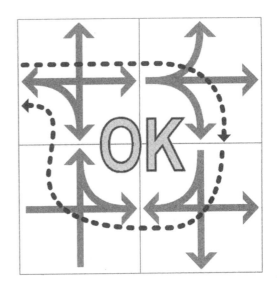

28. Paper Route

Deliver the local paper. Start at the upper left, follow the arrows and return to the upper right. For detailed instructions on Path Arrow mazes, see the section introduction on page 35.

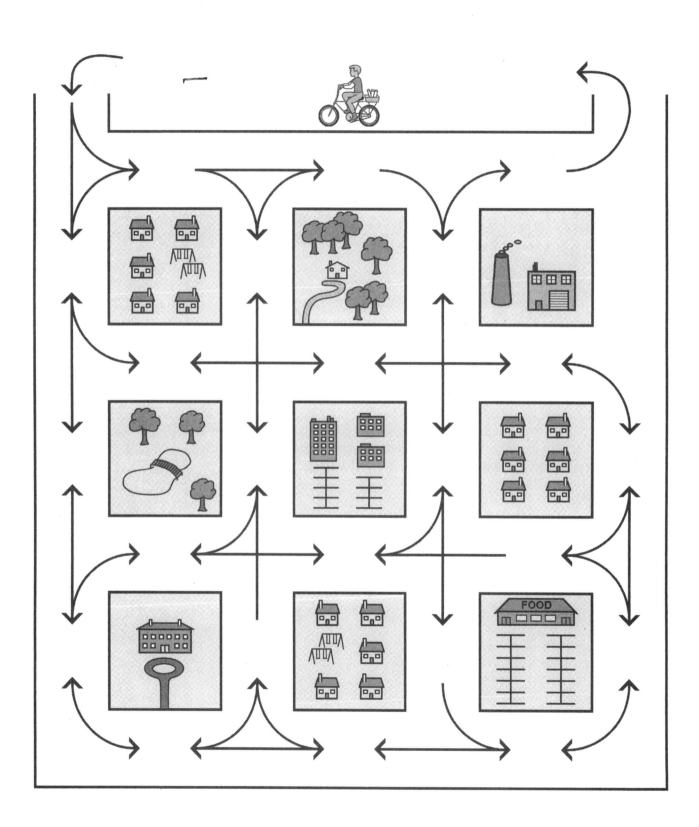

29. Beehive

Enter the honeycomb at the top left and follow the arrows that will lead to the bottom right. For detailed instructions on Path Arrow mazes, see the section introduction on page 35.

30. Gemstone

Start at one of the arrows in the center of the gemstone. Follow the arrows until you reach one of the six exit arrows on the outside of the maze. For detailed instructions on Path Arrow mazes, see the section introduction on page 35.

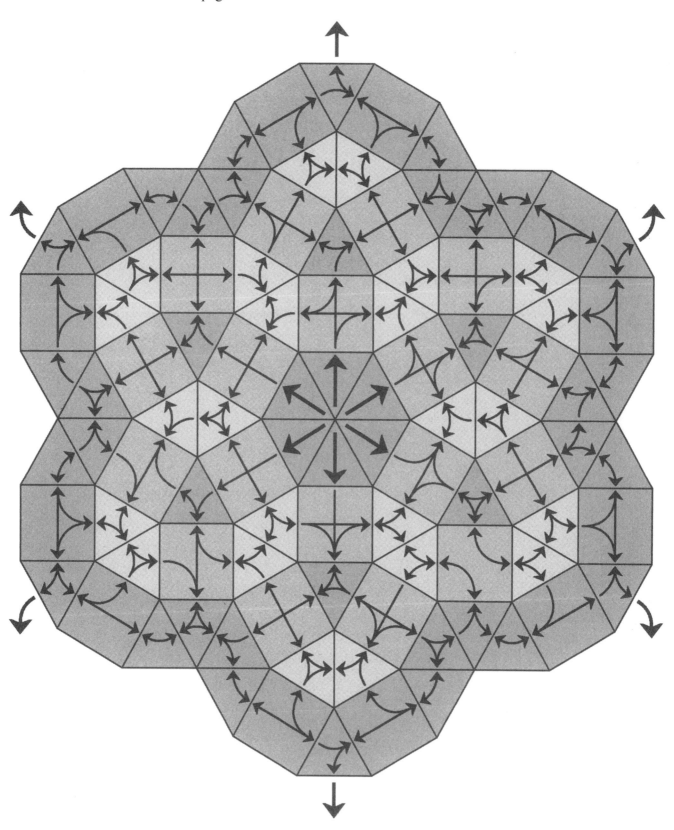

1. Construction 3-D

2. Construction 3-D – 5 x 5 x 5

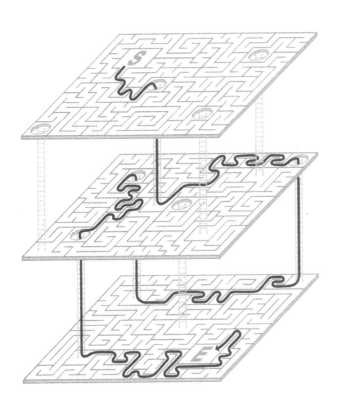

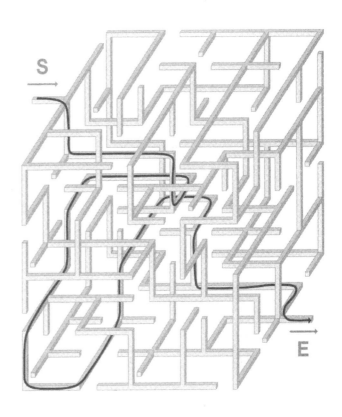

3. Three Planes with Ladders

4. Four-Dimensional Maze

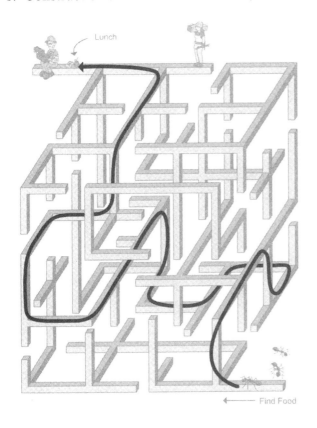

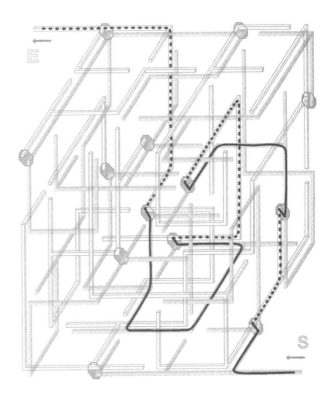

5. 3-D Walkways

6. Anthill

7. Deliver The Goods

8. Blood Flow

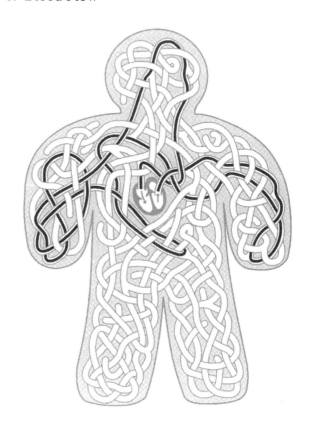

9. Weave

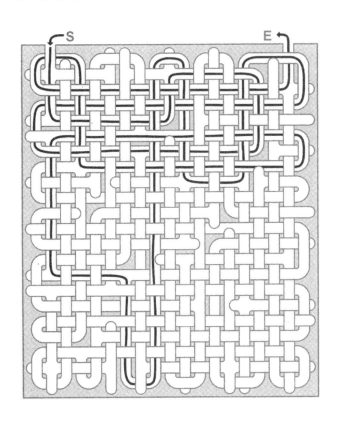

10. Commuter Madness

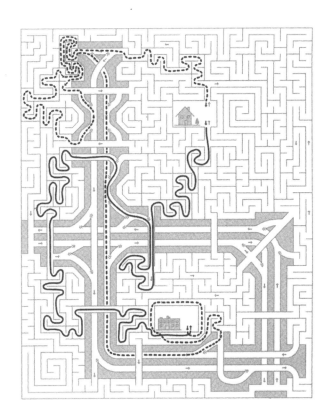

11. Cube Warm-Up

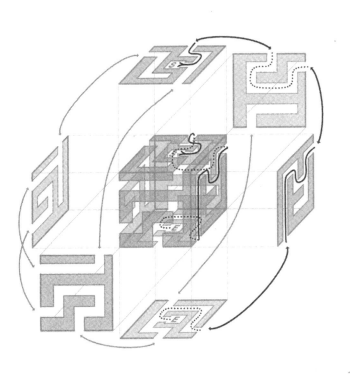

12. Cylinder Surface

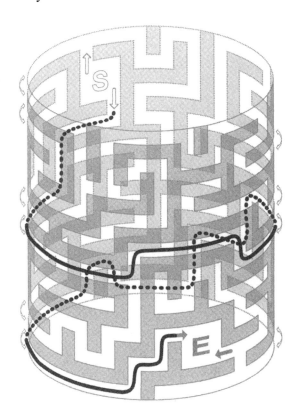

13. Die Surface

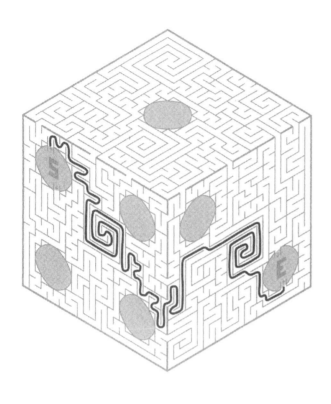

14. Cube Surface

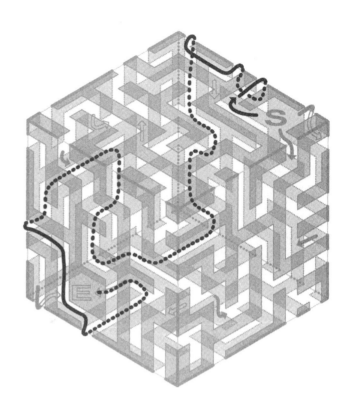

15. Cube Surface (4 mazes in 1) #1, #2 & #3

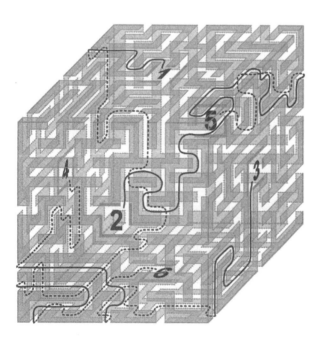

15. Cube Surface (4 mazes in 1) #4

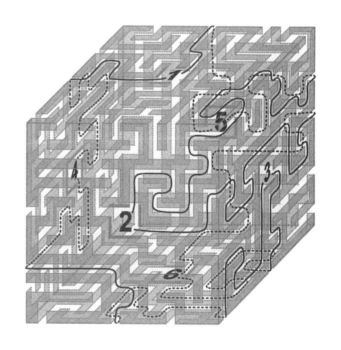

16. Easy As 1-2-3

17. Compass

18. Home Run

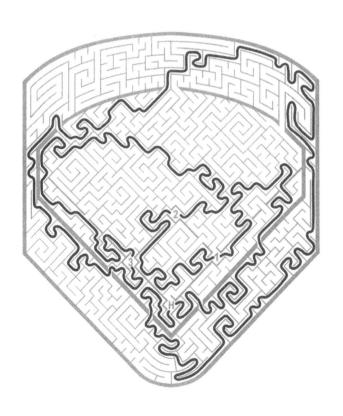

19. Cubes With Seven Stops

20. Pick Up Kids

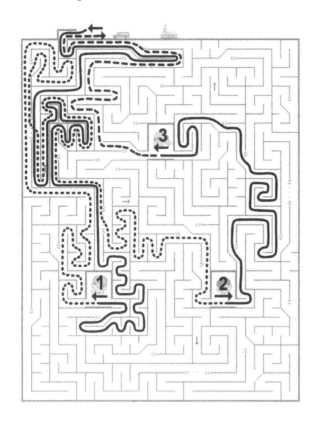

21. Jailbreak

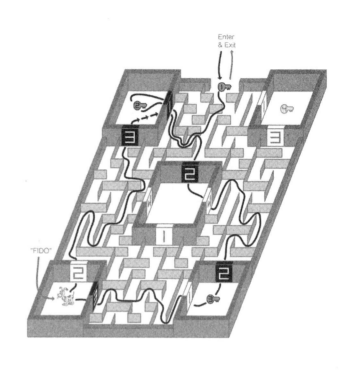

22. Mansion (First Half)

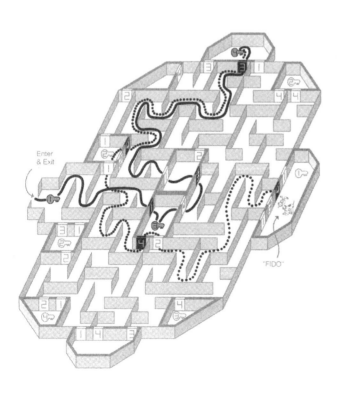

22. Mansion (Second Half)

44

23. Building Fire

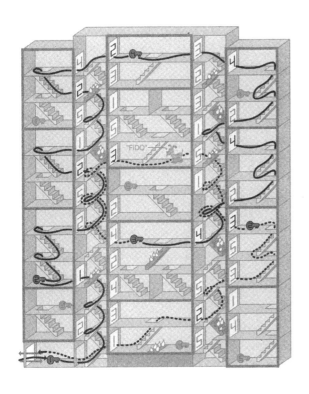

24. Chessboard

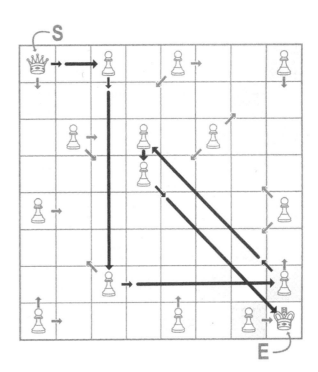

25. Trick Shot

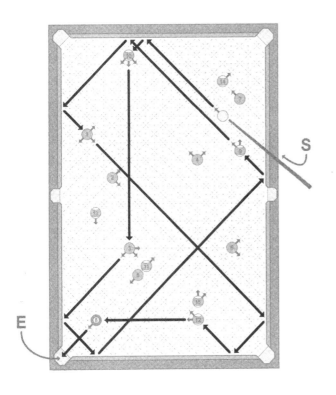

26. Hexagonal Arrow Maze

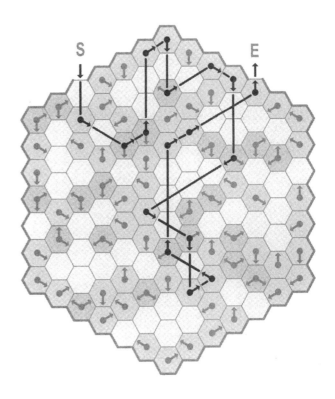

45

27. Lone Electron

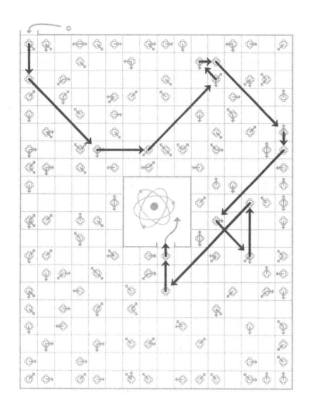

28. Paper Route

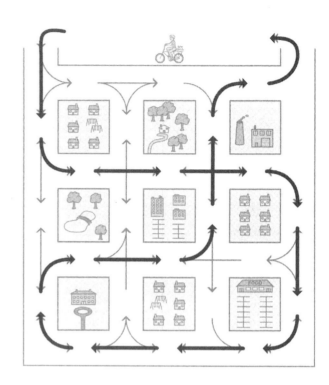

29. Beehive

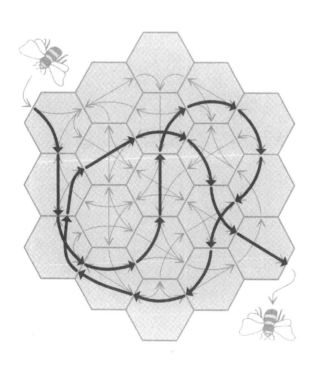

30. Gemstone

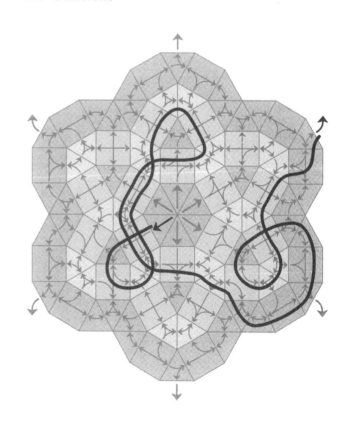